BRUCE TULLOH'S RUNNING LOG

The Complete Runner's Companion

by

Bruce Tulloh

PSL

Patrick Stephens Ltd,
Wellingborough, Northamptonshire

First published in 1986

British Library Cataloguing in Publication Data

Tulloh, Bruce
  Bruce Tulloh's running log: the complete runners
  companion.
  1. Running
  I. Title
  796.4'26   GV1061

ISBN 0-85059-844-3

Patrick Stephens Limited is part of the Thorsons Publishing Group

Printed and Bound in Great Britain by
Whitstable Litho Ltd., Whitstable, Kent

Personal Details

Name

Address

Phone No

AAA Registration No

Club

RUNNING RECORDS

Distance	All-time best	Last Year	This Year

THIS YEAR'S TARGETS

Beginners *(Mark Shearman)*.

Introduction

It is said that running is an addiction. I hope it is true, because nothing could be better than to be addicted to something which gives pleasure, benefits your health and gives you a lifelong interest. I have been running regularly for forty years, since starting as a schoolboy. In those days runners were freaks — now they are heroes. Whatever your level of ability, self-knowledge is an essential ingredient of success. To achieve the impossible, you must start from the possible. Once you know what you are capable of, you can set realistic targets for the next few months.

The reason that running has become so popular is that it is a direct expression of our own personalities. We are given a certain physical make-up, but it is up to us to develop it in the way we choose — or to neglect it. This running log should become the history of your own progress. In later articles you will find schedules for different events and distances, but these are generalized methods used by the average runner — whoever he or she may be. You are yourself, and have to find what suits you best. As the weeks go by, you should be able to relate the results you get to the training you put in. When you have a good run, look back over what you have been doing in the previous two or three weeks. If you get a strain or an injury, a look in the log will very probably tell you what brought it on.

Every three months you will find a page for review of training and results. If you are happy with your state of fitness, you can look over the past weeks and work out which kind of training is the most enjoyable and the most beneficial (not always the same thing!) If you want to go on moving up, then three months is about the right length of time for the body to adjust to each effort level. During the three-month period you can introduce one or two new features, but the overall volume should not change very much. If you are a ten-mile a week jogger, moving up to being a twenty-thirty miles a week runner, you should give yourself three months on the new level before even thinking about trying the forty-fifty miles a week which I recommend for the half-marathon runner.

Above all, a log is the place for reflection. You remember the good times and the bad, you learn from your mistakes and you draw inspiration from your successes. Without a record, you could lose your sense of direction, but now you have it, you can go as far along the road as body and mind are prepared to go.

May the next twelve months bring you all the fun and fitness you deserve!

Bruce Tulloh.

The One-person Experiment

Welcome to the world of running! Whether you are one of the new wave runners or someone who has been running since schooldays, there is always something to go for. Above all, it is something which can be enjoyed on your own terms, at the level which you choose. The ten-fold increase in the number of runners over the last decade has been accompanied by far more opportunity to compete. The first question you must answer, therefore, is 'what am I running for?' Do you want to be at the front or merely a little slimmer?

There are many good reasons for running, and you want to be sure what your aim is before you decide how much you are going to do. You may find, of course, that your aims change as time goes on. There has been more than one case of a woman taking up the sport to keep her husband company, with the hope of keeping her weight down at the same time, and then finding that she was better than him! One of these, Priscilla Welch, went on to run for Britain in the Olympics and is now a star of the American road circuit — at the age of forty!

If your reason for running is to get fitter and live longer, that need not prevent you from enjoying it. Sport of any kind should add to your life, not restrict it. The great thing about running is that it is under *your* control and done at *your* pace. You don't need a pitch, a referee, or even any other players. It is the cheapest sport you can do, because it needs so little equipment, and it can be done anywhere in the world.

What gives running perpetual fascination for me is that you never can know all the answers. The training which works for one person will not work as well for another, because we are all genetically unique individuals. Every one of us is a one-person experiment, and the experiment can go on for the whole of our lives.

Despite the foregoing, there are general principles of training which hold good for most people, and it is on these that I have based the schedules which follow. The marathon and half-marathon schedules are based on those I have written for *Running* magazine, and they have the advantage of having been used by hundreds of runners, many of whom have achieved their goals.

The others are based on schedules used by people I have advised over the past ten years. How do I decide the right kind of training? It comes mostly from my own experience, and on my knowledge of how much the average person is prepared to put up with.

When you decide *your* level of training, you must decide how much time you can afford to give or want to give. It is possible to spend all day on training, eating and resting, which is fine if you are a professional athlete, but for most of us one hour a day is about the maximum. Do not despair, on one hour's training a day you could reach top national level in any running event up to the half-marathon, if you had the basic talent. Of course, the only way you'll find out is by trying it.

In running, we start with the possible and achieve the impossible. As we get fitter we can do more training and as we do more training we get fitter. It is just up to you to say where you draw the line, when you reach a point where extra improvement is just not worth the extra time and effort. At each stage in your running, you can set yourself goals which are possible for you. You might start with 'running a mile non-stop'. A few weeks later the goal could be 'being able to run for half an hour', or 'being able to get round a ten-kilometre road race course'.

Covering the distance has got to come first, but for most people, the idea of running faster is not far behind. Being able to run faster than before is a sign of fitness, a sign that you have conquered your natural laziness and have raised your body to a new pitch of efficiency. With a little trial and error, you will find out which distances are best suited to your ability. This will reduce your choices, because you can now say: 'I am training to be better over a half-marathon' — or whatever your distance may be.

When you have got your distance, choose a few events to run in. For a few, competition is an occasion for winning prizes, fame, even large sums of money, but for most, a race is a chance to celebrate your fitness in the company of others. The longer the distance, the more friendly and supportive the runners are. In marathons, particularly, the feeling of friendship, of overcoming difficulties together, is tremendous.

As you get into running and make new friends, the next step is to join a club. Athletic clubs are mostly small, friendly, amateur affairs. Some cater for all branches of track and field as well as cross-country and road-running, but some are only concerned with the road and maybe the country. Some have tracks, some do not, but all of them welcome new members. They will not make great demands upon you unless you are very good — the club is a mutual self-help organization designed to help its members get more fun out of the sport. The big advantages are, firstly, moral support for your efforts and, secondly, a fund of experience on which the new member can draw. Don't expect to have everything done for you, though. In a club, as in life, the best way is to get involved and start doing things for yourself.

Steve Jones, world record holder for the marathon (*Mark Shearman*).

The Basics

One of the attractions of running as a sport is that you don't need any equipment or facilities to get started. You could make a start by going out for a one-mile walk in your lunch hour, in your ordinary clothes. Every now and again, break into a trot for a few yards, as if your were late for an appointment, then go back to a brisk walk. That's it! You have started training, strengthening joints, firming muscles, improving all-round fitness. Now is the time to check your weight. If you are considerably overweight you would do better to stick to regular walking, plus a regulated diet, until your weight has dropped and you are ready to run. If you are only slightly overweight, or normal, you can go straight into the Basic Jogging Programme. This requires only fifteen minutes a day, five or six days a week. The programme is as follows:

Days 1, 3, 5: Walk briskly for ten minutes, then turn round and jog back, pausing to get your breath when you feel like it.
Days 2, 4 and 6: Walk for fifteen minutes.

Stick to this programme for four weeks. After this time, you should notice the following changes:
1.   A slight drop in weight (perhaps a couple of pounds).
2.   You cover more ground in your fifteen minutes of walk-jog.
3.   You feel less tired after doing it.
    The next step is to increase the proportion of jogging in your fifteen-minute sessions. You could try alternating one minute's walking with one minute's jogging, or you could jog for five minutes, then walk for five, then jog for the last five. Keep on jogging three days a week, and increase the length of your walks to half an hour, twice a week. Now is the time to start thinking in terms of miles rather than minutes. The best place to do this is on a running track, which will be four laps to the mile. Run a mile at your normal jogging speed and see how long it takes. This gives you an idea of the distance you are covering in your regular outings.
    What equipment do you need? In the first few weeks, any old tennis shoes will do, but if you commit yourself to running

regularly, go to your local sports shop and try on some training shoes. Apart from that, any clothing will do, as long as you don't get too hot.

After eight weeks you should be able to manage to jog two or three miles at a time, three or four days a week. With a further four weeks of jogging a total of ten miles a week, you would be able to take part in short fun runs, not exceeding five miles.

The next stage is the move from jogger to runner. This implies, first of all, a commitment to running for its own sake. Whereas the joggers jogs to get fit, the runner runs in order to run faster and further. The sensible way to go is by improving the quantity first and then the quality of the running. We must work gradually up to twenty miles and eventually thirty miles a week. This, I think, is the minimum basic mileage for any serious runner. There may be weeks when, because of pressures of work or family, you cannot get out often enough and the mileage may drop to twenty, but if you can stick around thirty miles a week you will have the basis for successful performance over a wide range of distances. Starting from a basis of between ten and twelve miles a week in four outings, you should progress along the following lines:

Week 1	15 miles	(3 miles; 4 miles; 3 miles; 5 miles)
Week 2	15 miles	(3, 4, 3, 5)
Week 3	15 miles	(4, 5, 4, 5)
Week 4	18 miles	(4, 4, 4, 6)
Week 5	21 miles	(5, 5, 5, 6)
Week 6	21 miles	(5, 5, 4, 7)
Week 7	23 miles	(5, 3, 5, 3, 7)
Week 8	24 miles	(5, 4, 5, 3, 7)
Week 9	25 miles	(5, 5, 5, 3, 7)
Week 10	28 miles	(5, 3, 5, 3, 5, 7)
Week 11	30 miles	(5, 3, 6, 4, 5, 7)
Week 12	30 miles	(5, 3, 6, 4, 4, 7)

You can see that we are progressing in three ways — the number of runs per week, the total mileage and the distance of the longest run. For the latter you will need to put aside about an hour, so this will probably be at weekends, but most of the other sessions will be forty minutes or less. The exact distance of each run does not really matter — they can be estimated simply by how long it takes you, as long as you have a rough idea of your minutes per mile. It *is* important that you have different places to run, with different types of going.

What about pace? In the first few weeks I suggest that you do not worry at all about increasing your speed. You may well find, if you get into the habit of timing yourself round certain courses, that your times will improve without extra effort, just because you are getting fitter, but *don't* make every training session a personal record attempt — it only needs a few failures for you to get fed up with the whole business.

What about races? After six weeks on this plan, there is no reason why you should not try a race — any distance up to ten miles. Don't expect too much, but have a go and see how your time comes out. If you *do* race, give yourself one or two days of rest or very light jogging (two miles of shuffling) before returning to your regular programme. After following the twelve-week programme you could even tackle a half-marathon. Whether you do or not, you are now fully equipped to tackle the next upwards step.

Road Running

Although most races take place on the road, you should avoid training on the road all the time. At least one and preferably two days a week should be spent running on other surfaces such as playing-fields, park or woodland. The ideal situation is half the time on the road, half away from it.

On the thirty miles a week programme you will be able to run alright over distances of up to ten miles, but you are unlikely to reach your full potential. If you want to perform really well as a distance runner you should be thinking in terms of forty to sixty miles a week.

Until you find the pattern which suits you best, I suggest that you start with steady running up to your selected mileage, say fifty miles a week. As you are aiming at racing up to ten miles you will have one run a week, a slow one, over ten to thirteen miles, and with one day off you will have to run seven or eight miles on the other five days. I don't recommend twice a day training at this level — you are much better off doing one run a day properly. Of the five days, one should be over a short course, five or six miles. This means that on the other days you will be training for about one hour, and in this time you should alternate between hard and easy days. If you always plod along at the same pace you are not going to improve much beyond a certain point.

The only way you get better is by pushing yourself just that little bit harder. The right sort of speed is something around your six-mile racing pace, or maybe fifteen seconds a mile slower, in your hard runs, but in the easy ones there should be no sense of pressure at all, so the speed might be a minute a mile slower. There are many different systems in operation in your body and each type of training will bring improvement in different ways. Your training for the first six to eight weeks will look like this:

Sun	10–13 miles	Long easy run.
Mon	7–8 miles	Easy pace but with bursts up the hills.
Tue	5–6 miles	1–2 miles jog, then timed run over approx 3 miles, then 1-mile jog.

Wed	7–8 miles	Easy running, on grass, beach or paths.
Thu	5–6 miles	Brisk continuous run.
Fri	—	Rest.
Sat	5–8 miles	Race. If no race, try to do something strenuous but different.

Total 39–49 miles

When you have had some racing experience you will feel that you need to build up your weak points, of which sustained running speed is the most important. I have found that the most effective way of doing this is the road repetition run, over a distance long enough to get a lot of training effect, but short enough for you to operate at racing speed. This means a distance that takes you between three and seven minutes to run. Strength is built up through hill running and speed is acquired by repeated runs over short distances, from 100 to 400 metres.

When you have learned to incorporate these types of training into your week, you will be getting a lot more useful training done without much increase in either the mileage or the time taken. The pattern of hard days on Tuesday and Thursday, with a race on Saturday, can be followed unless it is a really important race, in which case you do your hard training on the preceding Monday and Wednesday, giving yourself two easy days. The pattern will look like this:

Schedule 5. Two-week programme before a 10-km race
Week 1

Sun	10–12 miles	Easy run.
Mon	6 miles	2-mile jog, two sets of 8 × 150 m on grass, 2-mile jog.
Tue	7–8 miles	Warm-up, then 5 × 1¼-mile circuit, timed. (6 minutes rest).
Wed	7–8 miles	Steady run, preferably off the road.
Thu	6 miles	Brisk run, with bursts up hills.
Fri	—	Rest.
Sat	9–10 miles	Minor race, plus 4 to 5 miles running about before and after.

Total 45–50 miles.

Week 2

Sun	12–14 miles	Easy run.
Mon	8 miles	Brisk run, including 8 to 10 × 300 m fast bursts.
Tue	6 miles	Easy run on grass plus strides.
Wed	5–6 miles	2-mile jog, then 2 miles, untimed, at fast speed. Five minutes rest, then one timed lap of the $1\frac{1}{4}$-mile circuit.
Thu	3–5 miles	Easy run.
Fri	0–3 miles	Rest or 3-mile jog.
Sat	6–8 miles	Race.

Total 40–50 miles.

The speed merchants — Peter Elliot and Seb Coe (*Nick Brawn*).

Speed Training

Whatever his or her distance, it is vital that the runner develops basic speed. The best place to do this is on a running track, because the improvements can be seen and measured, and the best way of doing this is to get involved in track races. The distances are mostly much shorter than those of road races, but the standard of running is much higher. The beginner should have at least six months of training behind him before trying track training, and the changeover from road training should be done gradually. The training pattern in the first year should look like this:

Day 1 Steady run, 5 to 7 miles.
Day 2 Interval training on track. 4 × 400 m at miling speed, with 1 lap (400 m) jog recovery, in under 3 minutes. 5 minutes rest, then repeat 4 × 400 m.
Day 3 Thorough warm-up, then 12 × 200 m approx on grass or sand, with 1 to 2 minutes rest between each. Speed should be appreciably faster than day 2.
Day 4 Easy run, 3 to 5 miles.
Day 5 1-mile jog, then 3 long bursts of 3 minutes fast running, untimed, on any surface, with 4 to 5 minutes' rest after each burst. 1-mile warm-down.

Every other week, substitute a time-trial instead of day 5. This time-trial can be over two laps, three laps or four laps of the track. The weather and track conditions, the time of each lap, and your personal reactions, should be recorded each time.

For the athlete who is already around five minutes for the mile or four minutes forty seconds for 1,500 m, we can assume a fairly high level of fitness and plunge straight into a pattern of interval training, repetition runs and speed work. When switching over to this pattern from a winter of cross-country and road, it is wise to introduce the fast sessions gradually. The pattern which follows is something which might in Europe be done in late April, with one of the first races at the end of two weeks.

Day 1 6 miles at a steady pace.

Day 2 2 miles warm-up, then 8 × 150 m up a slope (1 in 20), 8 × 150 m down the slope, 1-mile jog.

Day 3 Warm-up, 10 × 400 m in 72 to 73 seconds, with 200 m recovery jog (2 to 2½ minutes).

Day 4 6 miles fartlek.

Day 5 Time-trial over a favourite course, roughly 1 to 2 miles, with long warm-up.

Day 6 6 miles steady, then 6 × 150 m fast stride on grass.

Day 7 Warm-up, 3 × 1,000 m approx, 5 minutes rest between each.

Day 8 Fartlek run, 5 to 6 miles, with bursts on hills.

Day 9 Warm-up, 8–10 × 300 m, with 54 seconds recovery.

Day 10 Gentle jog or rest.

Day 11 Race.

Total (2 weeks) 45–50 miles.

Three rest days may be inserted as you wish.

What we are doing in this kind of training is improving your fitness so that it can cope with running faster. It is therefore suitable for anyone running three miles or more in races. If you have decided to go for shorter distances you really ought to think about the kind of speed training sprinters do. There are three distinct methods of improvement here.

The first and most essential is sheer muscular strength. Muscle power is the engine that drives your body forwards. You can build stronger leg muscles by such methods as weight training, or circuit training, done in a gym, or out of doors by resistance running. This means things like running up hills, running through soft sand or running with weights attached to you. Some sprinters practise running with a rope tied round their waists, pulling a tyre behind them.

At the same time as you are building strength, you should be working on mobility of the joints and flexibility of the muscles. Ten minutes a day, four times a week, spent on flexibility, will help increase your length of stride.

As the competitive season approaches you should be starting to bring these qualities together in sprinting sessions. A typical sprint session might start with twenty minutes of warming up and stretching, followed by three sets of 'sprint drills'. Each of these would involve running sixty metres six times. In each drill one particular aspect of the sprint action is accentuated — knee lift, arm drive, rate of striding, push off the ground, coming out of the blocks. Sprinting is a skill which has to be learned by repeated practice. Remember, whatever your distance, races are often won in a sprint finish!

Veterans cross-country (*Nick Brawn*).

Winter Training

Winter means different things in different places. In Florida, California and parts of Australia it simply means that the weather is cool enough to allow you to train really hard. In these climates you may be running your best races at this time, so will be following one of the racing schedules. What I'm talking about here is real winter, such as is found in Britain, Canada and the northern states of the US. This period can be divided up as follows:

1. Autumn. Time to build up the miles with un-pressured running, plus some cross-country races.
2. Mid-winter training. Survival during the coldest part of the winter.
3. Winter training. This is a hard training period which prepares you either for road running, up to the half-marathon distance, in the spring, or for the track season. Those who are set on the marathon would start with the winter training and move onto the special marathon work nearer the time.

These stages are examined in more detail below.

Autumn training When your racing season has finished it is a good thing to have two to four weeks of easy running, without going up to long distances or putting yourself under pressure. When you feel ready for proper training, you should try to put in a bit of everything. A typical week might look like this:

Sun	6–12 miles	Long slow run.
Mon	4–6 miles	Run out to hills, 12 × 100 m uphill, run back.
Tue	5–8 miles	Road run with club group, quite fast.
Wed	6 miles	Fartlek run, putting in fast bursts.
Thu	4–5 miles	Warm-up, then 3–4 miles at good pace.
Fri	—	Rest.
Sat	5–8 miles	Club cross-country race.

The total mileage here is only thirty or forty miles a week, but the beginner, and the average club runner, will get as much out of this as he will running sixty miles a week at a slow pace.

Mid-winter training   When the weather comes down really hard, you are faced with the problem of whether to go out and risk breaking a leg in the ice and snow or just to stay inside and get unfit. The latter is easy to do when bad weather comes around Christmas time, but if you have a few basic principles you'll be able to get through it.

My first principle is that it is better to survive the weather without getting ill or injured, rather than to persist with a rigid training programme. Even three of four weeks on a restricted mileage, half to two-thirds of normal training, won't do any harm. This means that you set yourself a lowered target of getting out, say, four times a week, and doing whatever the weather will permit. Make sure you have proper protective clothing, some of it reflective if you are training in the dark.

If you have a water- and wind-proof outer shell, hat and gloves and the right shoes, you can at least go for a steady plod, even in a snowstorm. Running through soft snow, in daylight, is good resistance training and makes a change from road work. If you are worried about your shoes slipping, wear boots. A good alternative is indoor circuit training in a gym. If you get the chance, cross-country ski-ing is very good training. You may have to avoid speed training in cold weather, but it's always possible to keep fit — the Finns manage it!

Hard winter training   A lot of big races take place in April or May. This means that your hardest training ought to be done in February and March. The following schedule is the kind of thing which might be done by a serious distance runner, with at least two years of training behind him:

Week 1

Sun	10–14 miles	Steady pace run.
Mon	8–9 miles	Warm-up, then 6 × 1 mile approx, timed, with 5 minutes rest between each.
Tue	8 miles	Fartlek, running 2 minutes fast, 2 minutes slow, then 1 minute fast, 1 minute slow.
Wed	5–7 miles	Run out to hill, then 8–12 runs up a hill 200 m long, run back.

Thu	5–7 miles	Warm-up, then 4–6 miles fast.
Fri	4 miles	Easy jog, morning or lunchtime.
Sat	7–8 miles	Warm-up, then club cross-country race.

Week 2

Sun	15 miles	Steady pace round a road circuit.
Mon	5 miles	Steady run in boots.
Tue	am 10 miles	Repetition runs at lunchtime, 4 × 1,200 m on grass (5 minutes rest between). Steady 4 miles in the evening.
Wed	8–10 miles	Steady pace with bursts, some fast.
Thu	7 miles	Road run, with hard 3-mile burst in the middle.
Fri	—	Rest.
Sat	6–10 miles	Race.

Total 98–114 miles (two weeks).

An additional morning run of 4 miles a day, Monday–Friday, would bring this training up to 70–80 miles a week — a good basis even for a marathon runner.

Week 1

Monday

Tuesday

Wednesday

Thursday

Afoot and light-hearted, I take to the open road, healthy, free, the world before me, the long brown path leading wherever I choose. Walt Whitman

Friday

Saturday

Sunday

Resting Pulse.............Body Weight.........Week's Mileage........

Number of sessions..:....Hard...................Total.....................

Easy ....

Week 2

Monday

Tuesday

Wednesday

Thursday

Fitness has to do with the quality of life, not the quantity of it.
George Sheehan

Friday

Saturday

Sunday

Resting Pulse..............Body Weight.........Week's Mileage........

Number of sessions......Hard...................Total.....................

Easy....................

Week 3

Monday

Tuesday

Wednesday

Thursday

The race we are running is against our weaker selves.   Bruce Tulloh

Friday

Saturday

Sunday

Resting Pulse..............Body Weight.........Week's Mileage........

Number of sessions......Hard...................Total.....................

Easy....................

Week 4

Monday

Steve Jones (left) and Dave Lewis (English cross-country champion) (*Mark Shearman*).

Tuesday

Wednesday

Thursday

We know not whom we trust, nor whitherward we fare. But we run because we must, through the great wide air.   Charles Sorley

Friday

Saturday

Sunday

Resting Pulse..............Body Weight.........Week's Mileage........

Number of sessions......Hard....................Total......................

Easy....................

Week 5

Monday

___

Tuesday

___

Wednesday

___

Thursday

___

The difference between commitment and involvement? Think of ham and eggs: the chicken is involved, but the pig is committed.

Martina Navratilova

Friday

Saturday

Sunday

Resting Pulse..............Body Weight.........Week's Mileage........

Number of sessions......Hard...................Total.....................

Easy....................

Week 6

Monday

Tuesday

Wednesday

Thursday

As I came over Windy Gap, they threw a halfpenny into my lap, for I am running to Paradise.   W.B. Yeats

Friday

Saturday

Sunday

Resting Pulse..............Body Weight.........Week's Mileage........

Number of sessions......Hard....................Total.....................

Easy....................

Week 7

Monday

Tuesday

Wednesday

Thursday

Does the road wind uphill all the way? Yes, to the very end.

Walter de la Mare

Friday

Saturday

Sunday

Resting Pulse..............Body Weight.........Week's Mileage........

Number of sessions......Hard...................Total.....................

Easy....................

Week 8

Monday

Tuesday

Wednesday

Thursday

Whenever I walk in a London street, I'm ever so careful to watch my feet.

A.A. Milne

Friday

Saturday

Sunday

Resting Pulse..............Body Weight.........Week's Mileage........

Number of sessions......Hard....................Total......................

Easy....................

Week 9

Monday

Marathon men.

Tuesday

Wednesday

Thursday

A fitness schedule must be respected, not worshipped.   George Sheehan

Friday

Saturday

Sunday

Resting Pulse..............Body Weight.........Week's Mileage........

Number of sessions......Hard....................Total.....................

Easy....................

Week 10

Monday

Tuesday

Wednesday

Thursday

Talent is developed in solitude.

Goethe

Friday

Saturday

Sunday

Resting Pulse.............Body Weight.........Week's Mileage........

Number of sessions......Hard...................Total......................

Easy....................

Week 11

Monday

Tuesday

Wednesday

Thursday

These high wild hills and rough uneven ways, draw out our miles and make them wearisome.   W. Shakespeare

Friday

Saturday

Sunday

Resting Pulse.............Body Weight.........Week's Mileage........

Number of sessions......Hard...................Total.....................

Easy....................

Week 12

Monday

Tuesday

Wednesday

Thursday

The true athlete is the one who runs year in and year out, always striving for the best.
John Walker

Friday

Saturday

Sunday

Resting Pulse..............Body Weight.........Week's Mileage........

Number of sessions......Hard....................Total.....................

Easy....................

Week 13

Monday

Taking drinks the Viking way (*Nick Brawn*).

Tuesday

Wednesday

Thursday

Training Tip: *Training is specific. If you are training for a fifteen minute race, you must get used to fifteen minutes of hard running in a session.*

Bruce Tulloh

Friday

Saturday

Sunday

Resting Pulse.............Body Weight........Week's Mileage........

Number of sessions......Hard...................Total.....................

Easy....................

Summary — Weeks 1–13

Mileage Total: Month 1   _____

Month 2   _____

Month 3   _____

Best Training Performances _____

_____

_____

_____

_____

_____

_____

_____

_____

_____

_____

_____

_____

The Half-Marathon

This distance has become extremely popular in the last couple of years — in fact, there are probably more people running this distance per year than the full marathon. The advantage is that it can be much more easily fitted into a normal life than the marathon, yet at the same time it offers a real challenge to your fitness.

I don't believe that you can run a *good* half marathon on what I call 'normal fitness training'. If you are a regular runner, your training probably enables you to cope with a ten-kilometre race, a five-mile cross-country or a two-and-a-half mile dash. At a pinch you might last out for ten miles, but if you go further you are likely to suffer. The choice lies between starting slowly and running at well below your 'natural' racing speed, or changing your training so that you can run the race properly.

Moving up

Let's assume that you are already running for thirty minutes, four times a week. The next essential thing is to increase your stamina so that your muscles can cope with a 100 minutes or so of continuous and steady running. As a guide to the speed you can expect to run, double your ten-kilometre time and add eleven minutes, so that you are running thirty seconds a mile slower for the longer event. To guarantee a successful half-marathon, I suggest the following guidelines:
1. Daily training runs of 5–6 miles.
2. Excluding the last week of 'tapering off', a weekly mileage of 25–30 miles during the month before the half-marathon.
3. You should be able to run 10 miles continuously on two occasions before the race.

Improving

Once you have a couple of half-marathons behind you, you will start to recognize your weaknesses and know what aspects of your training need improving. The human body is very adaptable, given time. For long distance events — ten kilometres and over — you can reckon to go on improving steadily for five years if your training is regular and progressive.

The secret lies in a gradual increase in the training load, improving the quality of the training as well as the amount. In the first year you might be able to run up to thirty miles a week, spread over five days. In the first few weeks, the pattern will look like this:

Day 1 6–10 miles Start easily, think about getting round, not about the pace.
Day 2   4–5 miles Warm up, then 2–3 miles fast.
Day 3   4 miles Steady pace, off the road if possible.
Day 4   5–6 miles Choose a hilly course and work up the hills.
Day 5   5–7 miles Warm up, then race over 3–6 miles.
Total 24–32 miles.

Without increasing the total mileage, you can improve in three distinct ways, but I suggest that you introduce these into your weekly schedule one at a time, as follows:
1. Increasing endurance. Every other week, go for distance on your long weekend run and one of your mid-week runs, so that you are doing, say, a ten and a seven. You can cut down the distance on other days.
2. Increasing running speed. In the weeks when you are *not* running higher mileage, substitute repetition runs on Day 2, making it a session of between four and six half-mile runs, run fast, with three or four minutes' recovery between each. On Day 3, try putting in several fast bursts of twenty to thirty seconds' duration.
3. Increasing toughness. On your hilly course, practise putting in fast bursts on hills. One day run fast up the hills and another day practise striding fast down the hills, relaxing and lengthening your stride.

Advancing
No top-class distance runner runs less than fifty miles each week (mpw) and most will be in the ten-miles-a-day category. For serious club runners, making the half-marathon their longest racing distance, fifty to sixty mpw, with a lot of good quality running, is much more effective than 100 mpw of slow running. It is more important to work on speed than endurance. As long as there is one session every two weeks in which you run for an hour and a half, the distance need not worry you.

In the half-marathon you are running eleven miles or more at a steady state, that is, as close to your maximum oxygen uptake as you can go without accumulating lactic acid. You must therefore do most of your good training at around your best ten-kilometre pace, over distances from half a mile up to two or even three miles in each continuous burst. This repetition work is tough, and you will have to bring it in gradually, but the serious runner should be able to cope with one set of long repetitions and one set of short reps each week, plus a race and some hill work. The training plan for a two-week period will look like this:

Day 1	8–11 miles	Warm up, then 4–6 × 1½-mile circuit, timed, with equal time recovery.
Day 2	6–8 miles	Easy running, off road if possible.
Day 3	7–9 miles	6–8 × 800 m on track, or 3 minutes on grass, with 3 minutes recovery.
Day 4	6–8 miles	Run round hilly circuit, working on hills.
Day 5	3–4 miles	Easy jog only.
Day 6	6–10 miles	Warm up, short race, warm down.
Day 7	10–13 miles	Steady pace run.
Day 8	6–9 miles	Road run, with two hard stretches of 2 miles run under pressure.
Day 9	5–8 miles	Easy running, off the road, a few strides.
Day 10	8–10 miles	Fartlek run, with a lot of one-minute and half-minute bursts.
Day 11	4–5 miles	Warm up, run 3 miles at good speed, but not flat out, then jog.
Day 12	3 miles	Easy jog only.
Day 13	15 miles	Half-marathon race.
Day 14	8 miles	Two short runs, the first very gentle not on the road, or walking.

Total (two weeks) 95–121 miles.

Going for the Marathon
Part 1: weeks 1–5

It's quite easy to break the world marathon record. All you have to do is cruise through the first twenty miles at a shade under five-minute-mile speed and then kick in with a last ten kilometres in under thirty minutes. Simple. The race is the easy part — you have the crowds, the cheering, and the cameras, and you can run as if there is no tomorrow. If you have got the training right, the race is just a formality, the final stamp in your passport to the land of the super-hero.

The training is the hard bit, because it is not just one day, it is weeks and months. Through all that time you have to balance your enthusiasm against your lethargy, your demands of work and home, your good days and your bad ones. The praise you get is for the race, but you earn it in all those lonely hours on the road.

Success in distance running is mainly a matter of mental strength, will power tempered by common sense. By success I mean achieving your potential. If you get the mental attitude right, the fitness will follow.

We are starting from the assumption that you have already got a year or more of training behind you and are maintaining your fitness with twenty to thirty miles a week. We can therefore start straight in with improving the quality of your running. There is one other assumption — that you are not afraid to compete. Most of today's top marathon runners are good over a wide range of distances, from 5,000 metres upwards. You should, on your marathon training be able to enjoy everything — a track 3,000 metres, a five-mile muddy cross-country, a ten kilometre on the road or an inter-club relay race. Being fit gives you more opportunities, and if you can run faster times over ten kilometres you can knock a lot off your marathon time.

For this reason, the first few weeks of the schedule do not have many long runs, but they include more good quality sessions than you would find in most marathon programmes. Once you start to run faster, we can move up to running further. In these schedules the week starts on a Monday and ends on Sunday, because most of the races are on a Sunday. If you race more often on a Saturday, or have your long run on that day, you'll have to adjust everything by one day.

The lazy-daisy plan

This is for the person who is prepared to make a big effort to get round on the day, but wants the minimum amount of training necessary for getting round in about four hours. My wife tried it, and it works!

Week 1 Run on alternate days. Two or three runs of 20 minutes each and one walk-jog of 6–8 miles.
Week 2 Three 20-minute jogs and one outing of two hours, walking and jogging.
Week 3 2 × 20 minutes, 1 × 30 minutes and one walk-jog of 8–10 miles (about two hours).
Week 4 3 × 20–30 minutes, one walk-jog of 2 hours.
Week 5 2 × 30 minutes, 1 × 20 minutes, plus a race of 6–10 miles.

The three-hour plan

Week 1

Mon	5 miles	Steady run, no pressure.
Tue	5 miles	Steady run, hilly course.
Wed	7 miles	Start slowly, increase speed in last 3 miles.
Thu	6 miles	One-mile jog, then put in several fast bursts, 150–200 yd.
Fri	0	Rest day.
Sat	7 miles	Cross-country or park run, steady.
Sun	8–10 miles	One hour or more, slow pace.

Total 40 miles.

Week 2

Mon	6 miles	One-mile jog, then five miles at a good pace.
Tue	5 miles	An easy run, you'll work hard tomorrow.

Wed	7–8 miles	Repetition session. One-mile jog, then 5 × 1-mile with 5-minute recoveries. Warm down afterwards.
Thu	4 miles	Easy running, preferably off-road.
Fri	0	Rest day.
Sat	7 miles	Cross-country with plenty of hill work.
Sun	12 miles	Add an extra mile or two, but still go slowly.

Total 41–42 miles.

Week 3

Mon	5 miles	Routine, untimed run.
Tue	4 miles	Fast and slow running, putting effort into bursts.
Wed	6 miles	Warm-up then a fast run over a course of 3–5 miles. This will be the basis for future comparison.
Thu	5 miles	Easy run off the roads.
Fri	0	Rest day.
Sat	7–8 miles	Cross-country run with efforts on hills.
Sun	8 miles	Find a race, or give yourself a hard 6-mile run. Warm-up and -down.

Total 35–36 miles.

Week 4

Mon	5 miles	Good pace around your usual course, but untimed.
Tue	4–5 miles	Easy run, some jogging and striding.
Wed	7–8 miles	Repetition session as week three. Your times should be faster.
Thu	5–6 miles	Easy run, off the road.
Fri	0	Rest day.
Sat	5 miles	One-mile steadily, then some road intervals.
Sun	15 miles	The first really long one, but you should be able to cope by now.

Total 41–44 miles.

Week 5

Mon	6 miles	Steady run, slightly faster than marathon pace.
Tue	6 miles	Easy run, off the roads.
Wed	6–8 miles	Jog to hill, then 30–40 minutes of hill climbs.
Thu	8 miles	Warm-up, then go at brisk pace.
Fri	0	Rest day.
Sat	8 miles	Warm-up, then 5–6 mile time trial.
Sun	10–12 miles	Steady run, marathon speed or slower.

Total 44–48 miles.

The long hard road.

Week 14

Monday

Tuesday

Wednesday

Thursday

Now bid me run, and I will strive with things impossible.

W. Shakespeare

Friday

Saturday

Sunday

Resting Pulse..............Body Weight.........Week's Mileage........

Number of sessions......Hard...................Total.....................

Easy....................

Week 15

Monday

Tuesday

Wednesday

Thursday

..about racing..there's no point in avoiding anybody, you've got to get out there and give it a bash.
Peter Elliott

Friday

Saturday

Sunday

Resting Pulse..............Body Weight.........Week's Mileage........

Number of sessions......Hard...................Total.....................

Easy....................

Week 16

Monday

Tuesday

Wednesday

Thursday

When you are fit, you fill your day; when you are unfit, you kill it.
                                                    George Sheehan

Friday

Saturday

Sunday

Resting Pulse..............Body Weight.........Week's Mileage........

Number of sessions......Hard...................Total.....................

                        Easy....................

Week 17

Monday

Tuesday

Wednesday

Thursday

I take the Gucci view about hard work on the practice field — long after you've forgotten the price, the quality remains.

Alan Jones, Australian Rugby coach.

Friday

Saturday

Sunday

Resting Pulse..............Body Weight.........Week's Mileage........

Number of sessions......Hard....................Total.....................

Easy....................

Week 18

Monday

Tuesday

Wednesday

Thursday

It is better to wear out than to rust out.
                    Richard Cumberland, Bishop of Peterborough.

Friday

Saturday

Sunday

Resting Pulse..............Body Weight.........Week's Mileage........

Number of sessions......Hard...................Total.....................

                    Easy.....................

Week 19

Monday

Tuesday

Wednesday

Thursday

You can't train the way I do and go out with girls.   Joaquim Cruz

Friday

Saturday

Sunday

Resting Pulse..............Body Weight.........Week's Mileage........

Number of sessions......Hard....................Total......................

Easy....................

Week 20

Monday

Club relay racing (*Nick Brawn*).

Tuesday

Wednesday

Thursday

Because runners are extremists by nature, they can sometimes be extremely wrong.
                                                                    Bruce Tulloh

Friday

Saturday

Sunday

Resting Pulse..............Body Weight.........Week's Mileage........

Number of sessions......Hard...................Total.....................

                            Easy....................

Week 21

Monday

Tuesday

Wednesday

Thursday

Most of the decline that comes with age isn't inevitable at all. It's caused by disuse.
Dr Kenneth Cooper

Friday

Saturday

Sunday

Resting Pulse..............Body Weight.........Week's Mileage........

Number of sessions......Hard...................Total......................

Easy....................

Week 22

Monday

Tuesday

Wednesday

Thursday

When is a man strong, until he feels alone?   Robert Browning

Friday

Saturday

Sunday

Resting Pulse.............Body Weight.........Week's Mileage........

Number of sessions......Hard...................Total.....................

Easy....................

Week 23

Monday

Tuesday

Wednesday

Thursday

We swing ungirded hips and lightened are our eyes. The rain is on our lips,
we do not run for prize.
                                                   Charles Sorley

Friday

Saturday

Sunday

Resting Pulse..............Body Weight.........Week's Mileage........

Number of sessions......Hard...................Total.....................

                              Easy....................

Week 24

Monday

Tuesday

Wednesday

Thursday

I'm not really a marathon man.   Steve Jones

Friday

Saturday

Sunday

Resting Pulse.............Body Weight.........Week's Mileage........

Number of sessions......Hard....................Total.....................

Easy.....................

Week 25

Monday

Tuesday

Wednesday

Thursday

Runners who train the same, stay the same.   Frank Horwill

Friday

Saturday

Sunday

Resting Pulse.............Body Weight.........Week's Mileage........

Number of sessions......Hard...................Total.....................

Easy....................

Week 26

Monday

David and Priscilla Welch (the day after she came third in the New York Marathon (*Nick Brawn*).

Tuesday

Wednesday

Thursday

Training Tip: *After a week off, two days training will get you back into shape, after two weeks off you will need one week's training to get back.*

Bruce Tulloh

Friday

Saturday

Sunday

Resting Pulse..............Body Weight.........Week's Mileage........

Number of sessions......Hard...................Total.....................

Easy....................

Summary — Weeks 14–26

Mileage Total: Month 1   _____

Month 2   _____

Month 3   _____

Best Training Performances _____

_____

_____

_____

_____

_____

_____

_____

_____

_____

_____

_____

_____

_____

_____

_____

Going for the Marathon
Part 2: weeks 6–10

When the going gets tough, the tough have got to get going. Very often, if you are planning on a spring marathon, the hardest training comes at the time when the weather is at its worst. MAKE SURE THAT YOU ARE PROPERLY EQUIPPED. This means having weatherproof clothing, which must have some reflective material on it if you are running in the dark. If the weather is so bad that you can't contemplate the full session, at least get out of the door. It is surprising how your attitude can change once you are warmed up and on the run.

The next few weeks of training are going to be tough, whatever the weather. Each time you come to a hard session, try to run a little faster than the time before. There are risks. In motor-racing jargon you are 'red-lining it' — pushing yourself harder while trying to avoid going over the top into exhaustion and injury. As a rule, the hard days alternate with easy ones. It is important that you do take these days easily, otherwise you will not recover from the hard sessions.

Most of the fast work is done at a speed much faster than marathon race pace. The short races and the time trials will also be faster than marathon speed, but there should always be one session a week where the pace is related to the race you are preparing for. This is the mid-week 'pace run'. It should feel like the marathon, running under a little bit of pressure, but not so much that it makes you breathless.

On the long runs it doesn't matter whether you start slowly and then speed up or start fast and slow down — in fact, it would be a useful experience to try both. It *is* important that you do these runs without stopping and if possible without walking, so that your body gets used to the prolonged non-stop effort. The races play an important part too, because races are quite different from training. You may be pleasantly surprised to find that your comfortable speed in a race is much faster than in training. This is fine, except that you are using up fuel more quickly, so you need to get used to this before the big day. Some runners rise to the occasion of a race, others are inhibited by it, but until you try it, you won't know.

Running in a few races will also give you an idea of the time you can expect in your first marathon. You can usually reckon that it will take you less than three times the time you get in a ten-mile race, so if you can get under the hour in a ten-miler, you are on course for sub-three hours on the big day. Better still is the estimate you get from doubling your half-marathon time and adding ten minutes, which means that our sub-three contender has got to be under one hour 25 minutes, at least for the half-marathon.

The lazy-daisy plan

Whatever your ability, these are going to be the most important weeks. Even the most idle marathoner must try to fit in three long weekend runs in the next five weeks. The easiest way of doing a long run is to do it in company, so get a friend or enter a race. Try to stabilize your mid-week running at three thirty-minute sessions a week. Occasionally you can do a twenty-minute trial instead, at a faster speed, to test your fitness. The weekend running should follow this pattern:

Week 6   Saturday or Sunday — try a 2-hour jog-walk in the morning, plus a 5-mile run in the evening.

Week 7   At the weekend, try to cover the half-marathon distance in training. You may have to walk some of it, but keep going.

Week 8   Take the plunge, enter a 10-mile race. Start at the back and concentrate on finishing — forget your pride!

Week 9   Try to repeat the run you did in week 7. You should find that it is now a little easier, and possibly faster with the same effort.

Week 10   If you have done all the long weekend runs recommended, confine yourself to one hour of steady jogging, otherwise do the one you missed.

The three-hour plan

Week 6
Mon	6–7 miles	Fartlek, not too hard, on grass.
Tue	8 miles	Repetition session: 4 × 1-mile with 5-minute recoveries.
Wed	6–7 miles	Steady run over hilly route.
Thu	5 miles	Road intervals (eg, 8 × 1-minute efforts with 2-minute jog recoveries.
Fri	0	Rest.
Sat	8–10 miles	Steady pace run.
Sun	13–15 miles	Long run, start easily.

Total 46–52 miles.

Week 7
Mon	6–7 miles	Easy running, with some strides, off roads.
Tue	6–8 miles	Steady pace, faster than marathon speed.
Wed	6 miles	Hill running, as Week 6 but not so much.
Thu	8 miles	5–6 mile time trial.
Fri	0	Rest.
Sat	8 miles	Steady run, about marathon pace.
Sun	10–12 miles	Start easily, work up to a good speed, finish fast.

Total 44–49 miles.

Week 8
Mon	6 miles	Slow and easy run.
Tue	6–7 miles	Fartlek, on soft going if possible.
Wed	8 miles	Repetition session: 4 × 1-mile with 5-minute recoveries.
Thu	6–7 miles	Steady run, bursts up hills.
Fri	6 miles	Nice and steady.
Sat	0	Rest.
Sun	13–15 miles	Race (10-mile or half-marathon).

Total 45–49 miles.

Week 9

Mon	7–8 miles	Choose a hilly course and throw in plenty of uphill surges.
Tue	10–12 miles	Pace run, slightly faster than marathon pace.
Wed	3 miles	Easy jog as 'active rest'.
Thu	7–8 miles	Road intervals: 8 efforts of 3 minutes with 1-minute jog recoveries.
Fri	7–8 miles	Steady run.
Sat	4 miles	Easy half-hour on grass.
Sun	13–15 miles	Start quickly and maintain pace.

Total 51–58 miles.

Week 10

Mon	8–10 miles	Good pace, with surges.
Tue	6–7 miles	Easy fartlek on soft going.
Wed	8 miles	Four repetition miles, with 5-minutes' rest in between.
Thu	5–6 miles	Steady run.
Fri	0	Rest day.
Sat	7 miles	An easy hour's run on grass.
Sun	18–20 miles	Start easily, build up to a good pace.

Total 52–58 miles.

Going for the Marathon
Part 3: weeks 11–15

The last few weeks before a marathon, and particularly the last two weeks, are the time for physical and mental tuning. This makes it difficult to prescribe a schedule which will suit everybody, because some people take longer than others to recover from a hard session. The over-forties and the under-twenty-ones should give themselves extra recovery time. Don't be hidebound by the schedule; take extra rest if you think you need it.

The key to the last weeks of preparation is 'bouncing back'. After each long or hard session, don't push it again until you really feel full of energy. That last phrase is literally true. It often takes several days for the muscles to replenish their stores of glycogen, that vital fuel, after a long run.

There are times when you will be running really hard, because through the past weeks you have been adjusting your body to a faster pace. The last interval session of Week 13 should find you running faster than ever before and the last long run, which must reach twenty miles or more, is going to push you into that region which the real runner must go through. Only by going into real fatigue and climbing back out of it will your body learn to cope with the special demands of a marathon.

In Week 14 you will be recovering and tuning. You should think about running fluently and economically, so that when you are running at your marathon speed you feel really comfortable. In the half-marathon run, one week before the race, you should be thinking of relaxation, keeping to the same effort level uphill and down. Don't try to make each mile time the same, think of equal *effort*.

To get everything right, there are one or two more things you can do. Adjusting your body clock is important. In the weekends before the race you should try to eat and train at the same times as you will on the day. You have conditioned your mind and your legs, so make sure that your digestive system is properly prepared. If possible, operate the same breakfast and training routine on the easy days before the race. Use the special marathon diet if you wish, but don't overeat the night before. Remember that your digestive system works more slowly when you are nervous.

Finally, check through your clothing and equipment. As well as your racing gear you may need protective clothing for when you finish, and if it is a big event you will need some old discardable outer garments to cover you after you have handed over your bag and your tracksuit. Thirty minutes of hanging about on a chilly morning could affect your performance if you are not prepared for it.

As you prepare yourself for the race you should be reinforcing your determination to keep going. Think of all the training you have done, all the time you have spent on it. Say to yourself: 'This is my day; I'm going all the way'.

The lazy-daisy plan

This, I'm afraid, is where the lazy runners suffer for their laziness. They have got to get *some* long runs in, and now is the time. The mid-week runs may be kept to a regular three or four thirty-minute outings a week.

Week 11   With four weeks to go, you have to try an 18-miler. This will be your longest training run, so get all the support you can.

Week 12   Take the mid-week runs gently, to recover. If you feel ready for it, try a half-marathon race at the weekend, or else a steady 8–10 miles.

Week 13   Try to repeat the 18-mile run. If you can get round this non-stop, you'll be alright on the day. Take drinks along the way, as you will in the race.

Week 14   At the end of this week you've really come to the end of the training. If you didn't do a half-marathon in Week 12 do one now, otherwise a steady 10 miles will do.

Week 15   Only one run this week! Put in a steady thirty minutes on the Tuesday or Wednesday before the race, but otherwise, just walk about, think about it, and store your mental and physical energy.

The three-hour plan

Week 11

Mon	8 miles	Pace run if feeling OK.
Tue	8 miles	Road interval miles, but with 4-minute recoveries.
Wed	12 miles	Steady, marathon-paced run.
Thu	7 miles	Short-burst fartlek (off road).
Fri	0–3 miles	Easy jog or rest.
Sat	6–7 miles	Very easy run off roads.
Sun	14–15 miles	Half-marathon or hard run.

Total 55–60 miles.

Week 12

Mon	8 miles	Easy run with a few strides.
Tue	7–8 miles	Time trial as week 8.
Wed	12 miles	As last week.
Thu	7 miles	Fartlek on soft going.
Fri	0	Rest.
Sat	7 miles	An hour's easy run.
Sun	20–22 miles	Your longest run. Be economical.

Total 61–64 miles.

Week 13

Mon	7 miles	One hour's easy run on soft going.
Tue	8 miles	Start slowly, put in surges if you feel OK.
Wed	8 miles	Road intervals: 5 × 1 mile with 5-minute recoveries.
Thu	10 miles	Fast (better than marathon pace) run.
Fri	6–7 miles	Fartlek on soft going.
Sat	0	Rest.
Sun	20 miles	Easy start, then marathon speed, but ease off in last 2 miles.

Total 59–60 miles.

Week 14

Mon	3 miles	Easy jogging and a lot of stretching.
Tue	8 miles	Start slowly, work to a good pace.
Wed	8 miles	Fartlek with a lot of short bursts.
Thu	12 miles	Steady run at marathon pace.
Fri	8 miles	Warm-up, then time trial as week 13.
Sat	3 miles	Easy jog, rehearsal for next week.
Sun	13–15 miles	Run strongly, but keep a little in reserve.

Total 55–57 miles.

Week 15

Mon	3–4 miles	Easy jogging on grass, plus stretching.
Tue	10 miles	Slowish pace.
Wed	5 miles	Easy fartlek.
Thu	5 miles	Warm-up, 3 miles at marathon pace, warm-down.
Fri	3 miles	Easy jog, at race time if possible.
Sat	3 miles	Easy jog in race gear and shoes.
Sun	26 miles	The race!

Total 55–56 miles.

The Runner's Diet

If there was a perfect diet for runners, which was superior to other diets and actually made you run faster, all top-class runners would be using it. In fact you find, if you look at a line-up of internationals, that they have all sorts of different diets. Take the Kenyans for example. Many of them belong to the Nandi tribe. Their native diet consists of a lot of milk — as much as a gallon a day. They eat eggs, but not much meat. Those of them who go into the Army or the Police Force go onto quite a different form of diet, containing a lot of maize flour, and those who go to college in America take up an American diet. These changes do not stop them being good runners; I am amazed that they have the flexibility to take the enormous changes in lifestyle and produce brilliant races all over the world. The lesson for us here is that the diet does not make the athlete. You will see vegetarians performing just as well as those who believe in enormous steaks.

On the other hand, a poor diet can affect you adversely. The difference between the runner and the average person is that the runner is testing his physical performance to the limit quite frequently, and if there is anything wrong with his health it will show up in his performances. For that reason you should have a few basic guidelines:

1. Eat at least three times a day. Small regular meals are best. If you go too long, more than about five hours, without eating, your energy reserves will run down and your blood sugar level will drop. This means that you will not be able to train very hard, except for marathons. Curiously enough, running on an empty stomach is good for marathon training, because it trains your body to release more fat more readily into the bloodstream. Running shorter distances, however, relies on the glycogen store, which needs to be kept up by eating.

2. Each main meal should contain the three basic ingredients of a protein source (meat, eggs, fish, milk, beans), an energy source (preferably a starchy food such as potatoes, bread or pasta) and a vitamin source (preferably fresh fruit or fresh vegetables). I'm not going to go into all the vitamins here, but as long as you

keep up your fruit and vegetable intake you should have no problems.

3. If you have to go a long time without a meal, it is better to have a bit of quick energy, in the form of a chocolate bar, or, better still, a muesli bar, than to do hard training on an empty stomach, which may be difficult.

4. To increase your recovery, it is a good thing to replace your muscle fuel reserves by eating soon after training. If you are not able to eat within an hour after the run, eat a bar of something to put back the energy.

5. Keep up your fluid level. Don't get dehydrated before you start training, and if the weather is hot, put the liquid back as soon as you've finished. This is the time when these special drinks are useful, but, personally, I find that a couple of beers do the job very nicely.

The marathon bleed-out diet

This originated in Sweden in the 1960s. I was one of the guinea-pigs when it was being tried out in this country, and I found that it was a big help for a low-mileage man. Ron Hill used it and became the world number one in the marathon in 1970. However, it doesn't work for everybody, and there now seems to be good evidence that the 'bleed-out' part is not necessary for those doing seventy miles a week or more, because they run down their fuel stores regularly in training.

For those who are planning to run a marathon — or any race of fifteen miles or more — this is what you should do. On the Tuesday, before the Sunday race, put in a long run, thirteen–fifteen miles, and then cut right down on carbohydrates for 48 hours. This means cutting out sugar, bread, potatoes and other starchy foods, but you can eat as much meat, vegetables, fruit and cheese as you like. Do very little running on Wednesday and Thursday, no more than four miles a day. You will feel pretty bad on Thursday, but that evening you can start loading up on starchy foods — hence the famous pasta-parties. You will probably eat a lot on the day after your fast, but I recommend caution on the day before the race. Eat a good meal, but don't make a pig of yourself, and have a short jog at some time during the day, so that your digestive system can work normally.

If you have followed the diet correctly, you will feel a bit heavy in the legs before the start, and even in the first few miles. This is because of the extra glycogen you are carrying, and the water which is stored with it. However, you will start to feel the benefits in the second half of the race, particularly after twenty miles, if you have judged your pace properly.

Alcohol and Smoking

Alcohol is a fuel, so long as you don't drink too much, the body will simply burn it off each day and you will have no harmful effects. Up to three pints of beer a day, or half a bottle of wine, will do no harm if taken after training.

Smoking *is* harmful. The nicotine affects the cilia in the bronchial tubes, the smoke particles irritate the lung and the tars can cause cancer. A little smoking — one or two a day — will have no discernible effect, but every additional cigarette will harm you more.

Week 27

Monday

Tuesday

Wednesday

Thursday

A record is made not by one effort of will, but by consistent training. By diligence and determination you can go beyond the limit of possibilities.

Emil Zatopek

Friday

Saturday

Sunday

Resting Pulse..............Body Weight.........Week's Mileage........

Number of sessions......Hard...................Total......................

Easy....................

Week 28

Monday

Tuesday

Wednesday

Thursday

How dull it is to pause, to make an end, to rust unburnished, not to shine in use.

A. Tennyson

Friday

Saturday

Sunday

Resting Pulse.............Body Weight.........Week's Mileage........

Number of sessions......Hard...................Total.....................

Easy ....

Week 29

Monday

Tuesday

Wednesday

Thursday

Everyone is allowed one stinker per season.   Peter Elliott

Friday

Saturday

Sunday

Resting Pulse..............Body Weight.........Week's Mileage........

Number of sessions......Hard....................Total.....................

Easy....................

Week 30

Monday

Victory (*Mark Shearman*).

Tuesday

Wednesday

Thursday

I'm in the sport because I love running. It's what I do best, it's what I was born for.
Steve Ovett

Friday

Saturday

Sunday

Resting Pulse..............Body Weight.........Week's Mileage........

Number of sessions......Hard....................Total......................

Easy.....................

Week 31

Monday

Tuesday

Wednesday

Thursday

The Press always ask a winning athlete: 'what does it feel like?' If you've got to ask, you'll never know.
                                                                    Harry Wilson

Friday

Saturday

Sunday

Resting Pulse..............Body Weight.........Week's Mileage........

Number of sessions......Hard....................Total.....................

                          Easy....................

Week 32

Monday

Tuesday

Wednesday

Thursday

The race is not always to the swift, nor the battle to the strong, but that's the way to bet.
                                                    Damon Runyon

Friday

Saturday

Sunday

Resting Pulse..............Body Weight.........Week's Mileage........

Number of sessions......Hard....................Total......................

Easy.....................

Week 33

Monday

Tuesday

Wednesday

Thursday

My strength is as the strength of ten, because my heart is pure.
A. Tennyson

Friday

Saturday

Sunday

Resting Pulse.............Body Weight.........Week's Mileage........

Number of sessions......Hard...................Total.....................

Easy....................

Week 34

Monday

Tuesday

Wednesday

Thursday

Poor men have grown to be rich men, And rich men grown to be poor again, But I am running to Paradise. W.B. Yeats

Friday

Saturday

Sunday

Resting Pulse..............Body Weight.........Week's Mileage........

Number of sessions......Hard....................Total......................

Easy....................

Week 35

Monday

The Adidas Marathon — V. Marot and S. McDiarmid (*Mark Shearman*).

Tuesday

Wednesday

Thursday

We must live on the alert, then we can get on with the business of being perfect.
George Sheehan

Friday

Saturday

Sunday

Resting Pulse...............Body Weight.........Week's Mileage........

Number of sessions......Hard....................Total......................

Easy....................

Week 36

Monday

Tuesday

Wednesday

Thursday

Running should enlarge your life, not diminish it.   Bruce Tulloh

Friday

Saturday

Sunday

Resting Pulse..............Body Weight.........Week's Mileage........

Number of sessions......Hard...................Total......................

Easy....................

Week 37

Monday

Tuesday

Wednesday

Thursday

Know then thyself, presume not God to scan, The proper study of Mankind is Man.
Alexander Pope

Friday

Saturday

Sunday

Resting Pulse..............Body Weight.........Week's Mileage........

Number of sessions......Hard...................Total.....................

Easy....................

Week 38

Monday

Tuesday

Wednesday

Thursday

Every dawn is a new contract with existence.   Amiel

Friday

Saturday

Sunday

Resting Pulse..............Body Weight.........Week's Mileage........

Number of sessions......Hard...................Total.....................

Easy....................

Week 39

Monday

Tuesday

Wednesday

Thursday

Training Tip: *No good runner wears brand new shoes in a race. Try out ALL your racing gear in training beforehand.*   Bruce Tulloh

Friday

Saturday

Sunday

Resting Pulse.............Body Weight.........Week's Mileage........

Number of sessions......Hard....................Total.....................

Easy....................

Summary — Weeks 27–39

Mileage Total: Month 1   _____

                     Month 2   _____

                     Month 3   _____

Best Training Performances   _____

_____

_____

_____

_____

_____

_____

_____

_____

_____

_____

_____

_____

The Health Hazards

The first thing to say is that running is a positive step towards greater health as well as fitness. In my experience, runners get ill less often, suffer less from depression (unless they have had a bad race!) and miss less time from work than inactive people. On the positive side, they can handle more work and get more into a day than sedentary folk, even taking into account the time which is spent on running itself. A number of research studies have shown that those who exercise regularly in their forties and fifties are much less likely to die of a heart attack than those who do nothing.

The first gibe which the new runner has to answer is on the lines of 'look what happened to Jim Fixx — all that running didn't do him much good, did it?'. The simple answer to that is that if Jim Fixx hadn't taken up running he might well have died at forty-two, like his father, instead of at fifty-two. For every man who dies while out jogging there are hundreds who die while in bed.

Running *is* stressful, that cannot be denied; it would not be much good for us otherwise. By giving our bodies a mild taste of stress we train them to cope with it. Not only does your heart become stronger, but with exercise your muscles become more efficient, the proportion of fat in the body becomes less and, if you are overweight, your weight will gradually return to normal. However, if you *are* overweight and unfit, there are precautions which have to be observed.

The beginner's schedule starts very easily, so that the muscles around the knees, ankles and hips, as well as the muscles of the back and abdomen, gradually get used to the extra strain. You should not be running long distances, particularly on the road, until your body weight is low enough and your joints strong enough to cope with it. If you take on a little more than you are ready for you may well get injured.

The fit runner seldom gets injured and the sensible runner is never injured for long. If you keep a note of how you feel after each run, the symptoms of impending injury can often be spotted. Frequent comments such as 'legs aching', or 'feeling heavy' tell us that you are training too hard. Remarks such as 'muscles stiff', 'strained right leg' have a very obvious message, but frequently I have seen them ignored by young and ambitious runners — indeed, I have ignored them myself — and what follows can be a pulled muscle, a stress fracture, or an inflamed tendon.

If you get pain somewhere building up while you are running, or you get pain after the run has finished, you should not run again until that pain has disappeared. If you are left with a slight stiffness or tenderness from a hard run, I suggest that you start by walking a mile. If the soreness has not increased, go on to jogging a mile very slowly, then, when you are thoroughly warm, go through a routine of stretching exercises. If, after that, you cannot run without discomfort, stop running for the day.

There are plenty of other ways of keeping fit which do not involve running on a damaged muscle or tendon. I would put cycling top of the list, with swimming a close second. In both cases your body weight is supported, yet you can take enough exercise to make your heart-lung system work hard and stay in condition. You should try to spend as much time a day on the alternative exercise as you normally spend on running.

If the injury takes the form of a slight pull in a leg muscle, followed by inflammation and soreness, the following self-treatment will get you back on the run in a few days:

1. Cool the painful area by putting an ice-pack on it (or a packet of frozen peas, wrapped in a tea towel). Hold the cold pack against the muscle for as long as you comfortably can.
2. Take a couple of aspirin (which have an anti-inflammatory effect) and rest the leg until the next day.
3. Put on walking shoes and walk steadily, but not fast, for thirty minutes, as long as this does not cause discomfort. At the end of the walk, apply the ice-pack to the pulled muscle and then try slow jogging on grass. If this can be done, keep it up for thirty minutes, then apply the ice-pack again.
4. The next day, spend fifteen minutes walking, then go through a prolonged warm-up. If you feel alright, carry on with normal training, but do only half your normal session. If you do feel pain after the warm-up, stop for the day.

If the injury appears in the form of a gradually increasing pain, say in the foot or the knee, do not try to 'run through it'. This may often lead to serious trouble. Give yourself a couple of days rest, and if that does not work, find out a 'physio' or a doctor who knows something about runners and get expert advice as soon as possible.

Common sense will help you avoid most injuries. Don't train on the road every day, and be sure you have some good training shoes. Vary the speed and distance of your training runs; work up to a maximum speed gradually; don't run hard when you are stiff or tired from the previous day and, above all, never race, or even train hard, until you have spent at least fifteen minutes on gradual warming up, loosening and stretching. If in doubt, ease up!

The London Marathon — it can be done (*Mark Shearman*).

Youth and Age

The schedules which I have produced in this and in other books are mostly for the fit adult runner, which generally means someone between the ages of twenty and thirty-five. I have made no distinction between men and women in the schedules, because I see no reason why a woman should not do the same training as a man, if she wants to run the same events. Although the average man will probably beat the average woman over most distances, the well-trained woman will beat perhaps three-quarters of the men in a mixed race. Age, experience and, above all, fitness, play a greater part in deciding what training a person should do.

Running for children

There is no reason why children should be prevented from running in races, as long as *they* can decide the pace they should run at, and can ease off when they feel like it. For this reason, it is best for most children that they run in their own age-group events. If they run against adults they may find themselves running too far and pushing themselves too hard. In some countries, where everyone is used to travelling on foot, a ten-year-old may be able to cope easily with a ten-mile run, but in urbanized societies the average boy or girl is just not fit enough for that. In Britain the AAA regulations state that you have to be at least sixteen to take part in open road races, up to a distance of fifteen kilometres and eighteen for races in the 25–50 kilometre range, which includes marathons. For training runs, I reckon that three miles is the maximum distance up to the age of thirteen; the thirteen–fifteen year-old can get used to distances of up to six miles. Over the age of fifteen it depends on the athlete and his experience, but they should be able to run for up to an hour, which means seven or eight miles.

You do find cases of young children, even seven-year-olds, apparently quite happy to run in ten-mile road races. I don't see anything wrong with this if the kid enjoys it, but the parents must keep a close watch for any signs of leg pains, and it is a good thing if they do a lot of their training on surfaces other than road. The human body was designed to run, but not on tarmac or concrete.

If a kid likes running and has talent, he should be encouraged to try different events and different distances. One person may start off as a good sprinter, then find that as time goes on he does better at, say, 800 metres. One of Britain's best 400-metre runners, Todd Bennett, started off running cross-country at school, then joined a club. When he tried different track events in the summer, the coach discovered that he was beating most of the sprinters in training. People develop at different rates, so don't give up just because you are not doing well after a few months of running. The first thing is to enjoy the sport and the second thing is to keep on improving.

The born-again runner

Many of the people turning out in road races have taken up the sport since the historic first London Marathon in 1981. Although the number of marathon runners now seems to have reached a plateau, the numbers running shorter distances continues to rise. Are there any special points for the over-forty newcomers? Will they be as good as those who have been running since they were at school?

The evidence seems to be that, even if you have not run for twenty years, you *can* reach the same level, given enough time and plenty of sense in building up the training. The classic case was that of the New Zealander, Jack Foster, who took up running in his late thirties and at the age of 41 won a silver medal in the Commonwealth Games marathon, running the distance in two hours and twelve minutes. At the age of fifty he ran close to two hours and twenty minutes — a time which is good enough to win many races.

Jack Foster's performances, and those of many other men and women who have come into the event later in life, show that it is the will which counts, not the age. Distance running performance does decline slowly with age, but the effect of training can largely offset this. The decline is very gradual — for a ten-kilometre race one might slow down at the rate of one minute in six years after the age of thirty-five, assuming that one kept on training at the same effort level. Someone who started from scratch, however, taking, say fifty-five minutes for a ten-kilometre or six-mile race at the age of forty, might improve by three minutes a year for the next five years and be approaching his peak at the age of forty-five or more.

The older runner will not go wrong if he gives himself time. He or she should not be running for quick results, but for fun, fitness and, above all, survival. This means that he should be happy to improve the training very gradually, staying at each level until he is fully adjusted to it. As you get older, it takes longer to recover from hard training and from races, and the schedule should be adjusted to allow for this. I reckon that one hard day and one long day is enough for me, at the age of fifty, and one race a month, but you should find your own level. If you want to race every week, that is fine, but do not expect to produce your best performance every time out. The things to remember are:

1. Have a good soak in a hot bath after your race.
2. Jog very slowly on the following day.
3. Don't start training hard again until you are free from aches and pains.

Seb Coe demonstrates flexibility (*Mark Shearman*).

Upwards and Onwards

You have come to the end of twelve months' training and competing. It has been fun, I hope, and you have made progress. What next? This is the time to review the progress and decide whether you want to go further, or whether you'll be satisfied with going round the same cycle again. Look at yourself critically. What running events are you best at? Which ones do you enjoy most? Do you want to do better?

So, you want to do better? Look at your record of races: was there a certain time of year when you ran better than before? Was this due to the training, the weather or your own attitude to running?

Look at your patterns of training and relate them to the races. Does one thing work better for you than anything else? Some people like a rigidly organized system, with plenty of timed work, others like to run as they please. Some thrive on long slow distance, some on short high pressure runs.

Perhaps, you have a bit of ambition and some idea of what training suits you? Are you prepared to put in a little more time and effort, not all the year round, but in preparation for certain events? You are? We're on the way.

If you know what distance of events suits you best, that obviously is at the centre of your training, but that shouldn't stop you enjoying the rest. The running world today is full of excitement, and if you don't mind getting beaten, there is so much to enjoy. Every runner at some time or other should have a dabble in some of these things: Orienteering — now a world-wide sport, but with its home in Scandinavia; Triathlon — best in Australia, California or Hawaii; Fell Running — in Scotland, the North of England, or for the really big ones, Switzerland's mountain races; cross-country in Britain or the north of Europe; track and road the world over.

If you had the time, the money and the energy, you could spend a lifetime taking in the great road races of the world — the 'City to Surf' in Sydney; the 'Bay to Breakers' in San Francisco; the 'Stramilano' in Milan; the 'San Sylvestre' in Sao Paulo; the 'Boston Marathon' — the list is endless.

Whatever your ambitions and your pocket, there is one challenge that lies ahead of us all — that of beating the clock — or the calendar. When you get into the veteran age groups a new world of opportunity opens up. The dividing line is over-forty for men, over-35 for women. Since the majority of races offer special awards in the veteran category, there are a good many in the running world who look forward to the birthday which most people dread. It doesn't stop at awards, either, because there are British, European and World championships for veterans, which are attracting more competitors every year.

So, whatever your age or your ability, there is something to look forward to. The next question is what you are going to do to prepare yourself for it. In your first two or three years in the sport you are going to run faster every year, because you are getting fitter, but then you will reach a 'plateau'. Provided that you have enough time the obvious way to improve is to run more miles a week, but that is not necessarily the best thing to do, unless you are going exclusively for the long distances.

The first thing you should do is examine your weak points. Score yourself out of ten for the following: leg strength, flexibility, sustained pace, stamina, finishing speed, coping with hills, ability to change pace, mental strength, frequency of injuries. Now decide which you most need to improve. Don't try everything at once — a couple at a time is plenty. The solution to the problems is mostly common sense — practise the things you are bad at — on top of the normal training you were doing before, but here are a few ideas:

Leg Strength   Use weights in a gym — a light weight, with a high number of repetitions.

Flexibility   Ten minutes steady stretching four times a week.

Sustained Speed   Regular sets of repetitions runs, at faster than your racing speed, over distances from 1 kilometre to $1\frac{1}{2}$ miles, eg, 6 × 1-kilometre, with 5 minutes' rest between.

For *Stamina* you, obviously, increase the length of your long runs, but also check that you have a sound diet. For sheer *Speed* you should try finishing off each run with a really fast 200 metres (and then warming down), as well as putting in regular sessions of 10–12 × 200 m of really fast running — say once every two weeks.

If you keep on getting injured, you have got to think hard to identify the reasons. Are you running too often on the road? Have you got the right shoes? Are you racing too often on inadequate training? Do you stretch thoroughly before running, and warm up properly in cold weather? Do you allow yourself to recover properly from marathons before hitting the training? If you are doing all the right things and still getting injured, you may have some imbalance in your legs or your spine, and you should look for professional help.

The solution to most problems lies in the mind. If you can find the patience to lay off when you have a minor injury, the mental strength to build yourself up gradually, and above all, the irrepressibility which every runner needs, you have a lot of fun ahead of you. Above all, learn from your mistakes and come back again — it's your life and your sport.

Zola Budd, world record-holder for 5,000 metres (*Mark Shearman*).

Week 40

Monday

Tuesday

Wednesday

Thursday

Lift up the hands which hang down, and the feeble knees.   Hebrews 12.

Friday

Saturday

Sunday

Resting Pulse.............Body Weight.........Week's Mileage........

Number of sessions......Hard...................Total.....................

Easy....................

Week 41

Monday

Tuesday

Wednesday

Thursday

Does the tearing tempest pause? Do the tree-tops ask it why? So we run without a cause, 'neath the big bare sky. Charles Sorley

Friday

Saturday

Sunday

Resting Pulse..............Body Weight.........Week's Mileage........

Number of sessions......Hard....................Total......................

Easy.....................

Week 42

Monday

Tuesday

Wednesday

Thursday

We shall never have any more time. We have, and we always had, all the time there is.
Arnold Bennett

Friday

Saturday

Sunday

Resting Pulse..............Body Weight.........Week's Mileage........

Number of sessions......Hard...................Total......................

Easy....................

Week 43

Monday

Tuesday

Wednesday

Thursday

..already 51, I couldn't expect to keep up 700–800 miles a month on my feet indefinitely.
Arthur Newton

Friday

Saturday

Sunday

Resting Pulse..............Body Weight.........Week's Mileage........

Number of sessions......Hard....................Total......................

Easy....................

Week 44

Monday

Tuesday

Wednesday

Thursday

Like everyone, I have bad times, but I don't expect every footstep to be a joy — I don't mind a bad run, because I know that all the runs add up to something positive.
Jim Fixx

Friday

Saturday

Sunday

Resting Pulse..............Body Weight.........Week's Mileage........

Number of sessions......Hard....................Total.....................

Easy....................

Week 45

Monday

On the Brighton Road (*Mark Shearman*).

Tuesday

Wednesday

Thursday

It is almost impossible to be fit and fearless without some sweating exercise most days.
Percy Cerutty

Friday

Saturday

Sunday

Resting Pulse.............Body Weight.........Week's Mileage........

Number of sessions......Hard...................Total.....................

Easy....................

Week 46

Monday

Tuesday

Wednesday

Thursday

It is not the beginning, but the continuing of the same until it be thoroughly finished, that yieldeth the true reward.   St Paul

Friday

Saturday

Sunday

Resting Pulse.............Body Weight.........Week's Mileage........

Number of sessions......Hard...................Total......................

Easy ....

Week 47

Monday

Tuesday

Wednesday

Thursday

I do not believe in athletics for the honours they bring, for all the athletic glory ever gained is not worth a month's ill-health.   Captain Webster

Friday

Saturday

Sunday

Resting Pulse..............Body Weight.........Week's Mileage........

Number of sessions......Hard...................Total.....................

Easy....................

Week 48

Monday

Tuesday

Wednesday

Thursday

By making ourselves fitter, stronger and more independent we are making ourselves better members of the human race.   Bruce Tulloh

Friday

Saturday

Sunday

Resting Pulse..............Body Weight.........Week's Mileage........

Number of sessions......Hard...................Total.....................

Easy....................

Week 49

Monday

Tuesday

Wednesday

Thursday

My advice to all is — seek out your gift — you will be sure to have one —
and develop it assiduously, for its own sake.   Percy Cerutty

Friday

Saturday

Sunday

Resting Pulse..............Body Weight.........Week's Mileage........

Number of sessions......Hard....................Total......................

Easy....................

Week 50

Monday

Tuesday

Wednesday

Thursday

We must be experts in ourselves. We must listen to our bodies.

George Sheehan

Friday

Saturday

Sunday

Resting Pulse..............Body Weight.........Week's Mileage........

Number of sessions......Hard....................Total.....................

Easy....................

Week 51

Monday

Tuesday

Wednesday

Thursday

On a flat road runs the well-trained runner, He is lean and sinewy with muscular legs. He is thinly clothed, he leans forward as he runs, With lightly closed fists and arms partially raised.   Walt Whitman

Friday

Saturday

Sunday

Resting Pulse..............Body Weight.........Week's Mileage........

Number of sessions......Hard...................Total......................

Easy....................

Week 52

Monday

Wendy Sly, Olympic silver medallist (*Nick Brawn*).

Tuesday

Wednesday

Thursday

Training Tip: *Run in the events you enjoy, not in the ones which people say you ought to do. It is a sport, after all.*   Bruce Tulloh

Friday

Saturday

Sunday

Resting Pulse.............Body Weight.........Week's Mileage........

Number of sessions......Hard...................Total.....................

Easy....................

Summary — Weeks 40–52

Mileage Total: Month 1   _____

Month 2   _____

Month 3   _____

Best Training Performances _____

_____

_____

_____

_____

_____

_____

_____

_____

_____

_____

_____

_____

_____

Training summary

Month	Week 1	Week 2	Week 3	Week 4	Odd days	Total

19   Total _____   19   Total _____   19   Total _____

Racing summary

Date	Race	Place	Time	Mile speed	Comments

Pace chart

Mile time	Two miles	Three miles	Five miles	Six miles	Ten kilometres	Ten miles	Half Marathon	Marathon
4.30	9.00	13.30	22.30	27.00	27.54	45.00	59.00	1.57.59
4.40	9.20	14.00	23.20	28.00	28.56	46.40	61.20	2.02.30
4.50	9.40	14.30	24.10	29.00	29.58	48.20	63.20	2.06.40
5.00	10.00	15.00	25.00	30.00	31.00	50.00	1.05.33	2.11.06
5.10	10.20	15.30	25.50	31.00	32.02	51.40	1.07.40	2.15.20
5.20	10.40	16.00	26.40	32.00	33.04	53.20	1.09.55	2.19.50
5.30	11.00	16.30	27.30	33.00	34.06	55.00	1.12.06	2.24.12
5.40	11.20	17.00	28.20	34.00	35.08	56.40	1.14.14	2.28.28
5.50	11.40	17.30	29.10	35.00	36.10	58.20	1.16.31	2.33.02
6.00	12.00	18.00	30.00	36.00	37.12	60.00	1.18.40	2.37.19
6.15	12.30	18.45	31.15	37.30	38.45	62.30	1.21.56	2.43.53
6.30	13.00	19.30	32.30	39.00	40.18	65.00	1.25.00	2.50.00
6.45	13.30	20.15	33.45	40.30	41.51	67.30	1.28.29	2.56.58
7.00	14.00	21.00	35.00	42.00	43.24	70.00	1.31.42	3.03.24
7.15	14.30	21.45	36.10	43.30	44.57	72.30	1.34.57	3.09.55
7.30	15.00	22.30	37.30	45.00	46.30	75.00	1.38.15	3.16.30
7.45	15.30	23.15	38.45	46.30	48.03	77.30	1.42.31	3.23.03
8.00	16.00	24.00	40.00	48.00	49.36	80.00	1.44.52	3.29.45
8.15	16.30	24.45	41.15	49.30	51.09	82.30	1.48.06	3.36.13
8.30	17.00	25.30	42.30	51.00	52.42	85.00	1.51.21	3.42.42
8.45	17.30	26.15	43.45	52.30	54.15	87.30	1.54.40	3.49.20
9.00	18.00	27.00	45.00	54.00	55.48	90.00	1.58.00	3.55.58
9.15	18.30	27.45	46.15	55.30	57.21	92.30	2.01.10	4.02.20
9.30	19.00	28.30	47.30	57.00	58.54	95.00	2.04.30	4.09.00
9.45	19.30	29.15	48.45	58.30	60.27	97.30	2.07.48	4.15.35
10.00	20.00	30.00	50.00	60.00	62.00	100.00	2.11.05	4.22.11
11.00	22.00	33.00	55.00	66.00	68.12	110.00	2.24.12	4.48.24
12.00	24.00	36.00	60.00	72.00	74.24	120.00	2.37.19	5.14.38

Useful addresses

Amateur Athletic
Association,
Francis House
Francis Street
London SW1P 1DL
Tel: 01-828 9326

Womens' AAA
Address as above

Midland Counties AAA
Devonshire House
High Street
Deritend
Birmingham B12 0LP
Tel: 021-773 1631

Northern Counties AAA
Studio 44
Bluecoat Chambers
School Lane
Liverpool L1 3BX
Tel: 051-708 9363

Welsh AAA, Hon Sec
'Winterbourne'
Greenway Close
Llandough
Penarth
South Glam CF6 1LZ

Scottish AAA, Hon Sec
25 Bearsden Road
Glasgow G13 1YL

Northern Irish AAA, Hon
Sec
20 Kernan Road
Portadown
Co Armagh
Northern Ireland

BLE (governing body for
Eire)
69 Jones Road
Dublin 3
Eire

The AAU of Australia
Olympic Park Athletic
Track
Swan Street
Melbourne
Victoria 3002

Women's Cross-Country
Association
10 Anderton Close
Bury
Lancs BL8 2HQ

To find a running club in
your area, get the address
of your county AAA
secretary from one of the
above associations.

Fell Running Association
Membership Sec
165 Penistone Road
Kirkburton
Huddersfield HD8 0PH

British Orienteering
Federation
41 Dale Road
Matlock
Derbyshire

New Zealand AAA
PO Box 741
Wellington

The Athletics Congress of
the USA
PO Box 120
Indianapolis
IN 46206

London Road Runners
Club
D. Billington, Hon Sec
1 Lynx New Road
Hampton Hill
Middlesex

Scottish Association of
Road Races
4 Couper Grove
Dunfermline
Fife KY11 5RD

Publications

For results of past events
and news of forthcoming
events, I recommend:

Athletics Weekly
344 High Street
Rochester
Kent ME1 1DT
(Available weekly from
newsagents)

Running Magazine
57–61 Mortimer Street
London W1N 7TD
(Available monthly from
newsagents)

Running Review
2 Tower Street
Hyde
Cheshire
(Available monthly)

The Orienteer
BOF Office
41 Dale Road
Matlock
Derbyshire